The Candidate and the Voter

A Novelette by Mitchell Doub

The Candidate and the Voter

Copyright 2020 by Mitchell Doub

ISBN: 978-1-71655-594-7

Printed in the United State of America

For

My Country (and Emily)

"When the people find that they can vote themselves money, that will herald the end of the republic."

Benjamin Franklin

The Candidate and the Voter

By Mitchell Doub

Colonel Gordon Alexander Hightower was quite accustomed to standing at attention, but this occurrence was special; because today, two weeks before his sixty-second birthday, he would receive the medal of honor. He stood tall and proud in his olive-green army dress uniform, flanked on his right by marine Sargent lance Atwood and on his left by civilian Nancy Speas, who would be accepting the honor on behalf of her father, army medic Joshua Bridgewater.

The early October morning was pleasantly cool with a few cirrus clouds turning the pale blue sky into a sugary shade of white. Gordon scanned the crowd of seated dignitaries, family members and press but saw no one he recognized. On this most important of days he was surrounded by dozens of people but was all alone. His mind strayed to thoughts of Margaret, his wife of almost

40 years and how he wished she was here. How ironic he thought, that we can put a man on the moon but we can't treat pancreatic cancer. Margaret had passed away a little over a year before and the disease was so advanced by the time they caught it she barely had time to fight at all. That's the thing with pancreatic cancer, stages one, two and most of three have few symptoms and stage four is almost always fatal. Gordon felt a bit of melancholy sweep over him as he glanced at the red roses, planted by Jackie Kennedy, (or her gardener at least), because roses had been Margaret's (he called her Peg) favorite flower. Had she still been alive Gordon would have hung around after the ceremony and surreptitiously picked a few. An indiscretion surely allowed a medal of honor recipient. As it was he would simply admire them... forget that, he would pick a dozen blooms and place them on Peg's grave that evening. She would like that.

"Ladies and gentlemen, Medal of Honor recipients, honored guests." Gordon snapped back to reality as an attractive blond spoke from the presidential lectern. " I am Sarah Alston, and I am the White House special events coordinator. It is with great honor and pride that I welcome you to the Rose Garden for today's Medal of Honor ceremony. The three recipients today have each distinguished themselves on the field of battle and exhibited great courage, heroism and selflessness in the execution of their duties. To this date, less than 3600 American servicemen and women have received their country's highest military honor. You're about to witness the rarest of all medal ceremonies. Ladies and gentlemen, the president of United States of America."

Gordon stood a bit taller as the president approached the lectern. The audience rose to their feet and welcomed the chief executive to his own backyard. He smiled, nodded and motioned for everyone to have a seat.

"Thank you Sarah and good morning my friends. I've only had occasion to do this a few times during my term but I must tell you that of all my duties, this is my most cherished. I like to think that every member of our military is a hero, keeping our nation safe and free. But the Medal of Honor is special. It is reserved for an elite group of individuals who, through acts of heroism, distinguish themselves in such a way that our nation takes pause to say, 'thank you.' Colonel Hightower, will you please join me on the platform."

Gordon took two steps forward, turned smartly to his left, climbed the three stairs and stood next to his commander in chief. The president put on his reading glasses, opened his

leather bound briefing notebook, and began to
read. "Colonel Gordon Alexander Hightower,
United States army, Special Forces, South Vietnam
theater of war. In November of 1971, in an action
code named; Operation Pegasus, Colonel
Hightower was leading his regiment on a relief
mission towards Khe Sanh where a Marine garrison
was completely surrounded. Colonel Hightower's
army group was ambushed by a large force of NVA
and Viet Cong troops heading south. For three
days, Colonel Hightower and his men courageously
repelled attack after attack as they waited for relief
that could not reach them. At one point, Colonel
Hightower received shrapnel wounds to both legs
and his left arm as well as a bullet wound to his
right hand. All the while, in total disregard to his
own safety, Colonel Gordon Hightower repeatedly
crawled across the field of battle and pulled five of
his wounded men to safety. Two of those five
brave soldiers survived their wounds and made it
home alive. Barely able to stand, bleeding
profusely and clinging to life himself, Colonel
Hightower refused to leave the field of battle until
the last of his wounded men were loaded onto the
medavac choppers that finally were able to get
through on the third day. It is with the greatest
respect and sense of duty that I award the Medal
of Honor to Colonel Gordon Alexander Hightower."

The president turned to his left and picked up the pale blue ribbon and golden medal and placed it around Gordon's neck. Gordon stood at attention as he shook the president's hand and the audience rose to give him a standing ovation. He glanced up to the sky and wondered if Peg could see him.

Later that night, Gordon parked his car, grabbed the bundle of red roses and slowly walked up to his wife's grave. " Hey girl." He said as he laid the six roses next to her marker. "These are pretty special, they came from the White House Rose Garden. I tried to get a dozen but some secret service guy thought six was plenty. Anyway, hope you enjoy them." He stood up and looked at the last vestiges of dusk. " Man, pretty sunset, isn't it?"

Gordon hung up his dress greens, walked into the living room and placed the Medal of Honor in the display case alongside the three Purple Hearts and the Silver Star. He sat down on his recliner and turned on the late news. As expected, most of the hour consisted of election coverage, specifically the presidential candidate pre-primary speeches.

"Well this should put me to sleep in short order."

Gordon took a sip of diet coke as he reclined back and turned up the volume a bit. A young female reporter was on-site in Iowa. "Democratic presidential hopeful and New York Governor Pete Stankowski kicked off his campaign today in Iowa and made big headlines with his tax promises."

About that time, Chloe, Peg's Mancoon cat jumped onto Gordon's lap. "Well hey buddy, where you been?" The cat purred and laid on her master's lap as he scratched her head. "Been a lazy day I bet." Gordon looked back at the Governor.

"My fellow Americans, I stand before you today with a promise. A promise that I will put to an end, once and for all to the unfair tax policies that have crippled the middle class of this country. It is time for this nation's richest citizens to pay their fair share!" The crowd roared in agreement. " I promise that I will overhaul our tax system so that any family making less than $30,000 per year will pay no Federal income taxes." Cheers from the crowd. "I will force the richest citizens of this country who have become wealthy on the backs of the poor and middle class to finally give back to this great nation and assume the responsibility to fund the social programs that our less fortunate need so badly!" Standing ovation this time.

Gordon shook his head and spoke to Chloe as the rubbed her back. "You hear that!? That's the kind of uninformed, empty crap that burns me up! He just told those people, hundreds of them, that he was going to lower taxes on one group and raise taxes on another. Too bad for him that all tax policy is in the hands of the House of Representatives. He either purposely just lied to all of America or he's ignorant. Either way he's not qualified to be president."

The disgusted Medal of Honor winner changed the channel, this time it was a Republican Senator from Virginia. "When I am president, I will cut taxes 20% across the board and put your hard earned money back into your pocket where it belongs!" The crowd jumped to its feet.

Gordon shook his head. " I'm all in fella, I need as much of my income as I can get, but why would you stand there and make some claim that you can't keep? The president can't cut taxes, you know that! Only Congress can for crying out loud!"

Gordon changed the channel again. A young reporter talked in the background as a split screen showed a Democratic presidential hopeful on the left and a Republican on the right. The reporter chuckled as he thought how smart he was at showing how opposite these two candidate's views were.

"As you can see, Democratic candidate Congressman Joyner, and Republican businessman Chase Miller are polar opposites when it comes to military spending."

The congressman spoke first; "I assure you Bryan, I have always been a proponent of a strong military, but we simply can't afford to continue to act as the world's policeman. If I'm elected president, I will force foreign governments to pay their fair share for the protection we provide and I will reduce our military budget by 10%, redirecting these funds for a much needed expansion of Medicaid."

The republican, Chase Miller, blurted in; "There you go Bryan, the liberal Democrat solution to any problem is to slash the military and increase welfare. I, on the other hand pledge a 25% INCREASE in military spending. We owe it to our brave servicemen and women to fully fund the weapon systems they need to keep us safe."

Gordon rubbed his forehead as if he had a headache. "I don't know if these guys are openly lying or if they just don't know any better. Even though they would be the commander in chief, all military appropriations come out of Congress. The president can neither increase nor decrease anything. Good grief!" Gordon slapped his recliner chair, which greatly annoyed Chloe and she responded by hopping off his lap and landing on the floor.

Gordon looked at the cat. "Sorry, but come on! People should vote for a candidate based on what the candidate can actually do, not on what they claim they can do, no matter how wonderful it sounds. These guys just make stuff up, and nobody even challenges them on it!"

Gordon got up from his chair, walked into the study and pulled a pocket size copy of the U.S. constitution from one of several oak book shelves. He looked at the small, white paperback book and ran the fingers of his right hand over the spine. He traced the outline of the American flag that emblazoned the front cover and opened the well-worn pages. He looked back at the TV and had an idea as the young reporter finished his sentence.

"Both candidates will hold rallies tomorrow morning in the DC area. Congressman Joyner will hold a rally at the Elks Club in Springfield at 9:00 AM and Mr. Miller will address supporters at the Arlington Hilton at noon. Both events are free and each candidate will take questions from the public." Gordon crossed his arms over his chest, stared out the back window and slightly nodded his head.

An early riser, Gordon was showered and shaved by 7:00 AM. His two bowls of Raisin Bran and glass of orange juice would get him through lunch and he grabbed a banana and Diet Cherry Pepsi for the morning drive. His second pair of dress greens were freshly pressed and he started for the front door. He turned off the alarm and paused as he began to turn the doorknob. He went back into the living room and faced the display case. A moment of indecision soon gave way to confidence as he took the Medal of Honor and placed it around his neck, he would need respect and deference today.

He arrived at the Springfield Elks club at 8:15 AM and stood in line to advance through security. A middle aged state trooper standing silent guard duty smiled and gave a salute as Gordan approached.

"Welcome colonel, it's an honor."

Gordon returned the smile and extended his right hand. "The pleasure is all mine, trooper...Gordon glanced at the troopers name badge. "Brighton."

"Thank you sir, and thank you for your service."

Trooper Brighton leaned in close, held up his right hand and displayed a very worn gold ring with an American flag on one side and a parachute on the other. "82nd Airborne sir."

Gordon beamed. "The pride of the armed forces. I've got lots of friends down in Bragg. You get back there much?"

"We do a squadron reunion every five years and I go down when family or friends have a kid graduating from basic."

"Next please." A twenty-something secret service agent motioned for Gordon to step forward through the metal detector. Gordon took out his keys, wallet and cell phone and placed them in the plastic dish on the table and began to remove his medal of honor. The young agent lightly touched Gordon's arm and leaned in closer. "No need sir, that can stay on."

Gordon nodded and smiled, slowly walked through the metal detector and retrieved his personal items. He entered the hall, roughly the size of a small high school gym and found a seat about halfway back on the right side. Most of those seated around him had red and white shirts, hats or buttons, proclaiming their support for Ellis Joyner.

"How long have you supported the congressman?"

Gordon turned to his right to answer the middle-aged lady with coordinated hat, shirt and button. "Actually, I don't really know who I'm going to vote for. I just wanted to hear what Mr. Joyner has to say."

"Wonderful!" The lady beamed. "I'm sure you'll be inspired, he's an excellant speaker." She smiled again as she admired Gordon's dress-greens. "You look very handsome in your uniform."

"Thank you ma'am, that's very kind."

"What branch of the service are you in?"

"I'm in the reserves now but I retired from the Army."

"My father was in the army, World War II, do you think you knew him? His name was Alfred Nichols. I think he was in Africa or Italy or somewhere."

Gordon chuckled, no ma'am, World War II was a little before my time and we had millions of men in arms so... Now if your dad was in Africa and Italy, any chance he served under general Patton?"

She beamed again. "Yes, I believe he did. He always watched that movie when it came on and tried to see if he recognized any of the places."

Gordon extended his right hand again. "You're the daughter of one of Patton's soldiers. I would love to shake your hand."

The lady was generally taken aback. "Well of course, but I didn't do anything."

"Any chance you could give my regards to your father?"

"We lost daddy a few years ago, a stroke."

"I'm sorry to hear that."

"Thank you. He lingered for several months but he couldn't swallow, or speak, or walk... strokes are such terrible things."

"Absolutely." Answered Gordon. "So tell me about congressman Joyner."

"Oh, he's wonderful, a few years ago my father had some difficulties with his VA benefits and a nice lady in Lewis' office took care of the problem and I've supported him ever since."

"I know that was a great relief. Do you know his thoughts on taxes, government spending, and foreign trade?"

The lady rolled her eyes. "Heaven's no, much too boring for me. My passion is social issues and I know Ellis will fight to keep government out of our personal lives."

Gordon nodded and paused. "That's certainly a good thing, how does he go about doing that?"

"Well, voting for the right laws I suppose."

Gordon nodded again. His thought was interrupted by the first speaker of the morning. Everyone turned and faced the stage. "Good morning Springfield!"

"Good morning!"

"Are you excited to be here!?"

"Yes!"

"Are you proud to be a democrat!?"

"Yes!"

"Are you going make Lewis Joyner the next president of the United States!?"

"Yes!!!"

"Cheers, shouts and clapping nearly raised the roof as Woody Guthrie's "This land is Your Land" blared through the rented six foot speakers. Congressman Joyner and his wife Lauren, bounded on the stage hand in hand and quickly made their way to the lectern. They beamed as they looked out at the now packed auditorium. The music faded as Lauren leaned into the microphone, clearly nervous, and blurted out; "Ladies and gentlemen, my husband, and the next president of United States, Lewis Joyner!"

Woody Guthrie was brought back to full volume as Lewis gave his wife a kiss and turned to address his adoring voters. "My friends and fellow democrats, I'm here to draw a line in the sand, and let it be known that that line was drawn today, in Springfield Virginia. A line that shall not be crossed. A line that ends women's fears about their right to choose, as I promise to only nominate judges to the Supreme Court that will uphold Roe vs. Wade!!!" The crowd lept to their feet and Woody blared from the speakers. "A line that promises that Medicare, Medicaid and Social Security will be fully funded for the next 50 years!!" Another roar. "A line that signals the end of a government that favors the rich and punishes the poor!"

Another huge ovation went up from the crowd as Gordon looked around the room to see the national news feeds from every channel imaginable. ABC, CBS, NBC, CNN, ABC, you name it, they were filming.

"When I become President I will level the playing field. My opponent, and friend, Pete Stankowski yesterday made a feeble attempt in Iowa to give tax relief to our nation's blue collar workers. But it is not enough. Come into the real-world Pete, come into the 20th century! He advocates eliminating Federal income taxes to those making under$30,000 a year." Several cheers filled the hall and Lewis put up his hands to silence the few Stankowski supporters. "It's not enough!" Now the rest of the crowd shouted their approval. "It's not enough. When I am president, any American earning less than $50,000 per year will pay no Federal income tax!"

The crowd erupted into pandemonium. The music blared, the crowd clapped along and Lewis and Lauren beamed. Gordon put his hand against his breast pocket and felt the familiar shape of the U.S. constitution. He couldn't decide if he was mad, puzzled or simply determined.

Lewis quieted the crowd. " Now, in the few minutes we have left I would like to answer some of your questions, if you have a question, please stand and one of these wonderful students from Georgetown will get you a microphone. Yes, the lady right here on the front row, your question please."

The closest Georgetown student rushed over to hold up the microphone. The lady began to speak but was overcome with stage fright, she could be heard through the mic. "Can't I just yell out the question, I hate microphones."

Lewis smiled, "Please use them mic mam, we all want to hear your question, it'll be fine. What's your name?"

"Oh, uh, Candace Whitaker, from Arlington, I, um, well, when will we know your list of possible Supreme Court nominees?"

"A great question Candace, we're putting that list together as we speak and it will be ready to be announced before the first debate. I'm sure you will be quite impressed as candidates from all backgrounds and social strata are being considered."

Candace blushed. "Thank you so much Congressman... I mean, Mr. President." The hall erupted.

Lewis pointed several rows back to his right. "Yes, the young lady in the red dress, what is your question?"

A Georgetown undergrad rushed over and extended the microphone. "I have not heard you speak much about climate change, it is my number one concern. Oh, Jennifer Gurley from Manassas."

"Thank you Jennifer, you hit on one of my passions as well. Please look at my voting record and you will see that I have voted over 20 times to reduce greenhouse emissions, I was a cosponsor years ago on the bill that banned CFCs, and as President I would never allow drilling in ANWAR!"

Standing ovation this time. Congressman Joyner basked in the Glory. Maybe he could pull this thing off… Maybe not. Lewis looked midway back to his left. "Yes the gentleman in uniform midway back, your question please."

A third Georgetown coed rushed to Gordon and leaned in so he could speak into the mic. "Gordon Hightower, and thank you for taking my question sir."

"You're very welcome."

Gordon touched the pocket holding the constitution, cleared his throat a bit and leaned closer to the microphone. "My question pertains to your tax proposal. Myself, being someone who made far less than $50,000 per year for much of my career would have been thrilled to keep more of my check."

Shouts of, "That's right! I heard that! Ain't it the truth!" echoed from around the hall. Gordon continued. "And I would certainly love to see taxes lowered for all working Americans… But there is a problem. All laws dealing with taxes and taxation, both lowering and raising, originate in the House of Representatives. The president cannot lower anyone's taxes, only Congress can."

You could have heard a pin drop. The smile on Lewis' mouth was in direct conflict with the look in his eyes. "Excellent question sir, uh, Gordon, right?"

"Yes sir."

"I don't want to debate a fine gentleman from our armed forces, but let's just agree to disagree and call it a matter of opinion."

"Actually sir, with all due respect, it is a matter of the U.S. constitution." Gordon had already pulled the well-read book from his pocket and turned to the first dog-eared section. "This is from sections seven and eight of the constitution: 'All bills for raising revenue shall originate in the House of Representatives. The Congress shall have power to levy and collect taxes… to pay debts and coin money. The president, actually cannot spend a dime, or raise or lower taxes by one cent unless Congress acts first."

Now would be the time when you could hear a second pin drop. The lady to Gordon's right scooted a bit further away from Gordon, maybe he didn't look so handsome after all. Lewis tried to rally and get this thing back on course, the problem was, how do you talk down to a decorated war hero. When he'd seen Gordon's Medal of Honor early on he secretly hoped the servicemen would have a question. How awesome it would look on the evening news to show himself addressing the question of a Medal of Honor winner. Lewis now wished a trap door would open on stage. He stumbled a bit with his words. "Well yes, that's true of course in the strictest sense of the law, but when I say I am going to lower or eliminate taxes I of course mean that I will encourage Congress to act."

A burly man in the back yelled out; "But that's not what you said!"

A low mummer began in the hall. Gordon spoke again. "I have made up my mind to vote for the candidate, and I urge everyone in this hall to do the same, who tells me... us, what he is going to do... that he CAN do, and make no more empty promises that directly contradict the U.S. constitution. I say this with all due respect sir."

"Well, thank you, of course..."

The speakers blared 'This Land is Your Land' again, some streamers fell from the ceiling and the lady that introduced Lewis took the podium again. "That's all the time we have for questions today, Congressman Joyner has a very busy schedule, thank you for coming and let's send Lewis Joyner off with a huge round of applause."

The room responded with a respectful sendoff but nothing near to what the welcome had been. Gordon could feel a thousand eyes staring a hole right through him. "Eff um, bullets hurt worse." Gordon joined the crowd as they made their way to the exits but he felt a hand grasp his right jacket sleeve. He turned, expecting to be verbally assaulted by a Joyner supporter, but instead was addressed by several media representatives.

"Stacy Blue from CNN…"

"Manuel Ortiz from NBC…"

"Do you have a moment?" The young woman from CNN asked.

"Uh, sure, I guess."

"What did you say your name was?"

"Gordon Hightower."

Manuel jumped in, "And you are an army veteran Medal of Honor winner?"

"Yes sir."

"What did you hope to gain today with your questions?"

"Did you hear my comments?"

"Yes sir, I have them recorded right here."

"Then before I answer, please tell me what you think I hoped to gain."

Stacy answered for Manuel. "It could have been interpreted as an attempt to kill the momentum of the rally."

"By quoting from the constitution?"

Stacy smirked as if to say 'Touche.'

Manuel spoke up. "Are you affiliated with another candidate?"

"No sir."

Manuel chose his words carefully, and slowly. "Surely the American people know that candidates are speaking in general terms…"

Gordon interrupted, but remained polite. "Promising to eliminate Federal taxes for anyone making under $50,000 per year is very specific. My goal was to come and hear for myself if a candidate for president would put forth an out and out misrepresentation, to respectfully challenge him on it and hope that he would from this day forward only make promises he has the power to keep. I intend to do the same thing with every single candidate… God willing."

"You'll make the same comments at other rallies?"

"Yes mam."

"Where again were you quoting from the constitution?"

"Sections seven and eight."

"Thank you."

"Absolutely."

Gordon started his car and popped the top on the Pepsi. He took a sip and enjoyed the cool burn as it made its way past his tongue. He put the transmission into drive and joined the row of cars heading for the exit. It was a few minutes before 11:00 when he arrived at the Arlington Hilton. He found a parking spot and made his way through security, only this time there was no trooper Brighton, only a couple of disinterested private security guards in the usual dark suits with even darker glasses.

This time Gordon found a seat a bit closer to the stage, but on the left side as he entered the ballroom. Gordon knew less about the republican candidate, Chase Miller, than he had known about Lewis Joyner. He opened the brochure that had been placed on his chair and began to read Mr. Miller's bio.

Chase S. Miller had graduated from Georgia Tech with a degree in structural engineering and earned his millions when he took over the reins to this father's construction business and began building prefab beach homes. Each home had 20 by 14 foot rooms that were constructed in the home facility near Charleston, South Carolina. The modular rooms would be trucked to the site and a rented crane would place the units on top of pre-sunk 12" by 12" pilings. A roof was built onsite and the beach home was finished in under a month. Chase had gotten the idea when he'd visited Disney world with his family and had stayed in the contemporary resort. Those rooms had all been prefabricated and trucked in. If it was good enough for Walt Disney, it was good enough for Chase Miller. The most interesting facet was that Chase was using his own money to fund his primary run. At the bottom of the pamphlet read in bold letters; "Chase Miller; the only candidate who cannot be bought!"

Gordon felt someone sit in the seat to his right, it was Manuel from NBC. "Colonel Hightower, I was hoping to see you here. I take it you will be asking a question."

Gordon smiled. "It depends."

Manuel returned the smile. "On if a promise is made that cannot be kept?"

"You just passed boot camp Private Ortiz."

Manuel shook Gordon's hand. "Now that I know what's coming I'll be able to savor the moment a bit more. By the way, behind the scenes you're the talk of the networks." He patted Gordon on the shoulder and returned to his post.

For his campaign, candidate Miller had chosen Bruce Springsteen's 'Born in the USA.' The song played in the background as Miller, his wife Charlotte and their teenage boys came down the center aisle, shaking hands as they approached the stage. Miller had wanted to go with maroon and ivory as his official colors but acquiesced to his staff demands and went with the more patriotic, red, white and blue. Gordon looked above the stage and saw a net filled with balloons of the aforementioned colors, all set for a modest balloon drop. The music got louder as the wealthy family took the stage. Chase went directly to the podium and seized the moment. "Hello Arlington, I'm Chase Miller and I'm the only presidential candidate that can't be bought!" The crowd lept to its collective feet and roared its approval. "Why would I spend tens of millions of my own money to run for president? Because candidates who accept huge contributions from powerful interests are bought and paid for and will have to return the favor during their administration. I will NOT be bought and I have NOT been paid for!" Roars of approval from the peanut gallery. "Furthermore, my promises are few but they are bold! One: I will reduce taxes, everyone's taxes by 25%!"

"Yes!"

"Number two, I will cut entitlement programs by 25% across the board!"

"Yes!"

"And number three, I will increase military spending by 25%! I call it the 25% solution!"

"Yes! We love it!" A chant rang out: "25% 25%! 25%!"

Chase smiled at the enthusiastic crowd and motioned for them to return to their seats. "I've got five more of these rallies to do today so let's hear from the people! Questions?"

A preteen boy was the first to leap to his feet and wave his arms. "Yes, the very enthusiastic young man in the front row!"

A staffer brought over the microphone. The boy was remarkably composed. "I love your campaign song but who is Bruce Springsteen?" The crowd broke out in laughter. "And shouldn't it be the 75% solution? You know, 25 plus 25 plus 25?" The crowd howled this time.

"Look little dude, I never said I was a math major, besides, 25% solution just kind of roles off the tongue." Applause all around. "Yes, the young lady in the Eagles' cap. You do know you're in Redskins territory don't you?"

"Sorry, born and raised in Philadelphia."

"Great city, tough fan base... Is it true y'all once booed Santa Claus?"

The girl covered her eyes and sheepishly replied. "No comment?"

"I thought so. So what's your question young lady?"

She clearly was emotional. "My father, my brother..." she paused to collect her composure as her voice began to quiver... "sorry... my father, my brother and two uncles all lost their jobs in the steel mills and coal mines of Pennsylvania. What are your plans to stop our bedrock Industries from going overseas?"

The crowd shook the room with applause. Chase looked the young woman square in the eyes and did not flinch. "My father built his construction business from scratch. He delivered a quality product at a fair price, yet he went through bankruptcy twice in his career. But you know what? Each time he got back up, dusted himself off and started anew. Someone once said, we aren't remembered for how many times we get knocked down, but for how many times we get back up." Cheers from the entire room. "I will institute a program where our nation's community colleges will offer a deferred tuition program where displaced workers can be retrained and repay their tuition after they gain employment again. But the best part is I will also offer a $10,000 tax credit to any business who hires a retrained, displaced worker at the going wage." Pandemonium. Chase was on a roll. "Yes sir, the army officer, thank you for your service and what is your question?" Chase smiled inwardly as he thought: "Come on soldier boy, throw me a softball and I'll knock it out of the park."

"Thank you Mr. Miller, yes I do have a question and it has to do with your 25% increase in our nation's military budget."

"Absolutely."

"Yes, thank you. Obviously I understand the need for a strong military, it is near and dear to my heart. It keeps our country safe and protects those in foreign lands who cannot protect themselves. My issue is not with your intent but with your ability to get it done."

Chase answered the question with confidence. "I assure you, I can get it done. As your Commander in Chief I will see to it that our military will see a 25% increase. They deserve it and they shall have it!"

Cheers. Gordon waited until the crowd settled down. "I totally agree, I've known military families who probably could have qualified for food stamps, but DESERVE has nothing to do with it. It's all about who can implement the idea. I applaud your passion for our military, but as Commander in Chief you cannot increase its budget by even one dollar. May I read from section eight of the U.S. constitution, and please note, it is not my intent to play a game of 'gotcha', because I think I'd enjoy having you as my commander in chief, but section 8 states the following: 'the Congress shall have power to provide for the common defense and general welfare of the United States... to raise and support armies... to provide and maintain a navy." Gordon closed the book. With all humility I must tell everyone in this hall that the President cannot increase the budget of the U.S. military. Only Congress can." There went that pin again. Manuel leaned back in his seat and scanned the crowd. "Wow." He whispered to himself.

Candidate Miller looked down for a second and then looked back at Gordon. "Do you question that I would advocate for our brave men and women in arms?"

"Not for a second. I believe you will be a firm advocate, but my only ask, and I ask this of all candidates; that when you address the American people that you differentiate between what you can do by the power of the constitution, and what you would like to see CONGRESS do by the power of the constitution."

Chase nodded his head, he knew when to fight back and when to simply count his losses."

"Fair enough, good sir, point taken."

Gordon returned to his seat and the crowd actually began to applaud. When the rally ended, Gordon headed towards the exit but was stopped this time by media representatives from every major station in the land. Manuel shook Gordon's hand and addressed his colleagues. "Ladies and gentlemen, allow me to introduce Colonel Gordon Hightower. Medal of honor recipient and retired U.S. army."

The ABC political correspondent was the first to ask a question. "Colonel Hightower, do you have time for a few questions?"

"Of course."

"Tell us please about yourself and your background."

"I'm retired army, as Manuel told you, I did multiple tours in Vietnam, I've served in the Pentagon and now I'm a colonel in the U.S. army reserve."

"What is your educational background?"

"I have an undergraduate degree in political science and a graduate degree in U.S. history.

"What schools did you attend?"

"Undergrad, James Madison, grad school, College of Charleston."

"Where are you from?"

"I was an army brat, so you name it, I'm from there. Born in fort Benning, Georgia."

"How old are you?"

"Born in 1930 so I'm 62."

The CBS correspondent raised her hand and chimed in. "Michelle Witherspoon, CBS. Colonel Hightower, why exactly are you attending these rallies? This is the second event in less than 4 hours that you have attended and each time you have been called on to ask a question and each time your question has brought a halt to the flow of the event. Is that your goal?"

"Michelle, right?"

"Yes."

"What if I told you I would sell you a great car for ten thousand dollars. It was exactly the car you'd been looking for and you were thrilled to have finally found it. You give me the ten grand and I tell you I will deliver the car. We shake hands and it is a good faith agreement. After a while you call me up and ask when the car will be delivered and I say that I didn't actually have the car but I know where one is, in fact Manuel has a car but I don't really know what kind it is, or what color, the condition or the miles. I just know it's a car. I tell you if I have the time I'll give Manuel a call and see if he'd be willing to part with his car. Now remember, I have your ten grand, you may, or may not end up with a car and as it turns out, you should have been going to Manuel looking for a car in the first place. Now, how would you feel?"

"Like I've been scammed."

"Exactly. I made a claim that I had little power to keep but I got what I wanted, now the only way you're gonna' get a car is if Manuel steps in. Now, the ten thousand dollars represents the people's vote. I am the presidential candidate, the car is a political promise made by the candidate during the campaign and Manuel is Congress.

"Michelle's eyebrows lowered a bit."

" Then why am I asking to buy a car from you?"

"You shouldn't be." Gordon grinned and pointed to Manuel. "He's got the car, you need to go to him directly."

"Like bypassing the middleman?"

"Not exactly, the President isn't really a middleman, he just doesn't have the legal right to sell you that call. Or, in the greater conversation, doesn't have the legal right to raise and lower taxes, spend the people's money, pass legislation, etc. Those powers reside solely with Congress."

The members of the media were either writing furiously or recording Gordon's every word with their handheld recording devices. One of the other reporters nodded and raised his hand. "Could we have your phone number Colonel?"

Gordon looked at the now sizable crowd and smiled at Manuel. "Manuel has it. I give him permission to pass it along to those of you that he feels he can trust with someone else's personal information. He nodded at his new friend and after a second Manuel returned the nod, turned to his rivals and held up his black address book. "OK folks, bidding starts at $100." Manuel turned back towards Gordon and smiled. "Just kidding."

Gordon had heard that the set of a national television show was purposely kept on the cold side to keep the guests from sweating under the hot lights, but the 62° that greeted him on the set of 'Meet the Press' made him wish he'd brought his gloves. Gordon sat patiently as the young makeup girl gave his face a bit of color and took an occasional sip from his Diet Coke. As Gordon was nearing the end of his first ever make-up session, Tim Russert, the second year host of the top rated news show took the seat to his right.

A middle aged male makeup technician quickly walked over and began to work on the TV personality. Russert had been host of the show for a little over a year and enjoyed it immensely.

"Good morning Mr. Russert."

"Hello Tony, how's your weekend?"

"Very well, finally got all the holiday stuff done. And you?" Tony quickly placed a small paper bib around Russert's neck and began to apply a bit of makeup base. Russert turned to his left and extended his right hand. "You would be Colonel Hightower."

Gordon shook Russert's hand and immediately decided he liked the newsman. "Yes sir Mr. Russert. Good to meet you."

"The pleasure is all mine. I must say that I've become quite a fan of yours over the past week."

"So have I."

"Me too." The two makeup technicians voiced their support while never missing a beat. Julie, the female technician began to powder Gordon's nose. "My father says you are his new hero. He's retired military by the way."

"Oh? Which branch?"

"Navy."

"He still approves of me?"

"Absolutely... Well, as long as Navy wins the football game this year."

Gordon laughed. "Tell your dad he has nothing to worry about this year, I think the Middies will go home happy."

Russert closed his eyes as he leaned his head back a bit. "I can't remember the last time I saw two politicians put in their place so adeptly." Russert pulled off his bib, stood up and grinned at Gordon. "Congratulations, see you on set."

Gordon took a sip of Coke as he saw the red light come on the nearest camera. Russert smiled and looked into the lens. "I guess you'd have to be hiding under a rock to not recognize the gentleman across the table, welcome Colonel Hightower."

"Thank you Tim, it's a pleasure to be here."

Russert addressed the over two million viewers once again. "Colonel Gordon Hightower, a veteran of two tours in Vietnam, the recipient of three purple hearts, the Silver Star and most recently the Medal of Honor, and now, political rally icon, or pariah," he smirked at Gordon, "depending on your side of the microphone during these events, has agreed to join me today and chat a bit about the often boring topics of presidential elections and constitutional powers. Some heady conversation subjects Colonel, what gives?"

Gordon, a bit more nervous than he had anticipated, took another sip from the black and red can. "I am not on a mission to rain on every politician's parade, as one young reporter suggested."

"Would that be a bad thing?"

"Depends on a politician."

"And on the parade." Russert interjected. "I've watched the tape of both the rallies you attended but just in case our viewers have not, let's take a look."

The tape rolled on the two rallies and after a few minutes the red light came back on the nearest camera. Russert was all smiles. "I must admit, the first time I saw these, I cringed at the awkward silence that followed your questions, but now, seeing these cuts for the third time, it makes me kind of happy, I can't help but smiling. I think we would all agree that Chase Miller handled the moment better than Congressman Joyner."

"I would agree, but I assure you it was never my intent to embarrass either, I'm sure they are fine men, I merely wanted to clarify a few minor points."

"Minor is an understatement Colonel Hightower, you've touched on a point that most Americans never even gave a second thought but is actually at the bedrock of our political system: the role of each branch of our Federal government, and in this case, most importantly the specific role and powers of the President of the United States. I have read the sections of the constitution you quoted and you're absolutely right. The president can neither raise nor lower taxes, he or she cannot spend the people's money nor adjust the size of the military by raising or cutting funding. Why does this seem like such a novel concept?"

"You know, I have always had a love for history, that was my major in college actually, and one of my minors was political science. The constitution and understanding the roles of the President, of Congress, of the Supreme Court, come second nature to me. I've got to frequently remind myself that not everyone else shares my passion for civics. I think that we all are so busy in our lives, our careers, the care for our families, that we all have little time left to learn about seemingly mundane subjects. We just vote for who we like or who we think we can trust and leave it to them to handle it from there. I know very little about decorating a home, buying gifts, planning vacations, so I asked my wife to handle those things, and she did it wonderfully. That's what we do with our elected officials, we ask them to handle the tasks we don't feel qualified to handle ourselves. But somewhere through the years the powers and responsibilities of the three branches of our governments have become blurred and candidates make claims they simply cannot keep. Hence my attendance at these rallies."

Tim nodded and smiled. "Were you nervous?"

"Not really, I've addressed large crowds many times before. I was more nervous coming on this show, but when you think about it, it's just you, me and the crew."

"And two million people."

"Like I said, it's just you, me and the crew."

Both men chuckled. "OK, let's… The seven or eight of us, continue our casual conversation."

"OK."

"We heard you speak at the rallies about what the President can do, tell us, constitutionally what he CAN do."

"I was hoping you'd ask me that. The first thing to remember is that most of the President's duties are foreign in nature. He or she is the head of our government and represents us to the heads of other governments. He and his Secretary of State are our official emissaries, negotiators if you will, with foreign powers. Now if you follow the constitution in direct order, beginning with article two, section one, the President's first duty and power is to preserve, protect and defend the U.S. constitution. That first duty is what led me to attend those rallies because how can a potential president preserve, protect and defend the constitution if they: 1. don't know it or, 2. purposely distort it."

"Good point."

"Section two addresses military powers: the President is to be commander in chief of all branches of the military. He or she shall have the power, with the consent of the Senate, to make international treaties, nominate ambassadors, public ministers, Federal judges and consoles and judges of the Supreme Court. Once again provided two thirds of the Senate approves. Section three states he or she should advise Congress on the state of the Union. He or she is to receive ambassador's and other public ministers. He or she shall see to it that our country's laws are executed and is to commission all the officers of the United States." Gordon stopped and took a sip of coke.

There was a brief silence as Tim waited for Gordon to finish. "Please continue."

"I can't, that's it... Check that, if the Vice President resigns, dies or is removed the President may nominate their successor."

"That's it? Those are all the powers of the president?"

"Yes. Now, there is considerable power through cabinet departments such as Education, Interior, etc, but those named are his constitutional powers."

"So to summarize:" Tim began to count of on his fingers. "He or she is the Commander in Chief, they represent us before other governments, they must protect and preserve the constitution…"

"And defend."

Tim nodded and smiled. " And defend. They can suggest treaties, nominate Ambassadors, Federal judges and Supreme Court judges… Hoping that the senate approves. He receives ambassadors, informs Congress on the state of the Union, sees to it that our laws are enforced, commissions officers, appoints his Cabinet and nominates the Vice President's replacement."

Tim paused for a moment and stared at Gordon. "Colonel, that's not a very long list."

Gordon chuckled. "No it's not. The writers of our constitution were all British citizens but they didn't even have representation in Parliament. They saw the dangers of being subject to a government with a very strong central head and wanted no part of it for a new country. They purposely limited the power of our chief executive and placed significant checks and balances upon the President to prevent him from becoming essentially a king. Now, I'm not going to say that we have a weak head of state, after all, he or she yields the might of the greatest military in the world, but the true domestic power in this land lies in the hands of Congress, specifically with the House of Representatives."

"And quickly, what are the powers of the House of Representatives?"

"To raise revenue, to collect taxes, to pay our nation's debts, to provide for the common defense and welfare of our nation, to borrow money, to regulate commerce with foreign nations and among the states, to regulate naturalization, to regulate bankruptcies, to coin money, to regulate the postal service, to punish crimes committed on the high seas, to declare war, to raise and support a military and to call forth the National Guard."

Tim nodded. "Wow, that IS significant power. And what about the Senate?"

"The senate has the power to try all impeachments, it negotiates with the House of Representatives on taxation and spending and approves or rejects legislation passed to it by the House. The Senate approves treaties, Ambassadors, public ministers, consoles and judges submitted by the President."

"A short but important list."

"Yes it is."

"And that leaves…?"

"The Supreme Court is the judicial power of our country. Cases begin at the local level and as they are appealed, and if accepted, they can be finally judged by the Supreme Court. Ultimately it is the responsibility of the Supreme Court to settle legal cases that make it to their docket and to decide whether laws passed by Congress are constitutional."

"Again, a short but important list."

Gordon nodded and took a sip of Coke. "All other powers not given to the Federal government by the constitution are given to the States or to the people directly."

"That's it?"

"That's it."

Tim smiled and looked at his over two million viewers. "Civics 101 by Colonel Gordon Hightower. Back in a minute." The camera's red light turned off and Tim turned in his chair. "Good stuff Colonel, you know your constitution."

"Thanks."

"Do you mind if we explore some other topics?"

"Sure, what do you have in mind?"

"The national debt, immigration, gun control, foreign trade, global warming."

"Absolutely."

The red light came back on and Tim addressed his audience again. "We've had an excellent lesson on the roles of our government, I think it might be interesting to get an ordinary American's thoughts on the issues of the day. "Colonel Hightower…" Tim turned to address his guest. "A recent article in a national news magazine stated that by the year 2020 our nation's debt will exceed Twenty trillion dollars and that interest on the national debt will consume anywhere between 20% and 40% of our Federal budget. Thoughts?"

Gordon smiled and chuckled. "A few. You've kind of hit my hot button right off the bat. Federal spending has no real cap, if the government runs out of money they simply pass legislation to raise the debt ceiling and then print more money. It would be like each month you and I calling our credit card company and asking for an increase on our credit limit, and the company never saying no. Soon we'd get to the point where our credit card debt is greater than our annual income, greater than the equity we have in our home, greater than the cash we have in our retirement account and bank accounts… We'd be totally upside down with no possible hope of paying off the debt. Our Federal government is in that exact situation. We spend twenty to thirty percent more each year than we bring in and we will never… I repeat NEVER be able to pay down twenty trillion dollars. And as the debt grows the portion of the budget that pays the interest and debt service will continue to grow, thus reducing what is available for other programs, unless…"

"Unless…"

"We greatly raise taxes, greatly cut spending, or print mountains of new money. None of these options, at least in my opinion, are realistic."

"Is there a way out?"

"Maybe." Gordon took a deep breath and let out a sigh. "Do you believe you pay enough in taxes already?"

"Yes."

"Me too. This is not an income problem, this is a problem with spending. We must cut the size of the Federal budget until receipts equal spending and then maintain a yearly balanced budget. Now personally, I believe the Federal rate should be 10% and the top state rate should be 10%."

"For everyone?"

"Yes."

"What about the poor?"

"I would be willing to make a concession and have a gradually reduced rate scale for those under the poverty line."

"But everyone would pay income tax?"

"Yes, everyone should pay something, even if it's just 1% of their income. Each citizen should have the motivation to vote for candidates which advocate for the lowest taxes possible, not the highest. It's common sense."

"How would you decide which programs are cut?"

"I wouldn't. Cutting $10.00 from the pentagon budget would literally take an act of Congress. Cutting $10.00 from education, from interior, from social programs, you name it would each take major political capital and would result in hundreds of fights and bickering like we've never seen. The answer, in my opinion is quite simple:

fight one battle and win it. Introduce legislation that reduces the entire Federal budget by 5% each year for seven years and we end up with a balanced budget. Now remember, that is 5% this year, and 5% more next year and so on."

"But wouldn't people suffer?"

"Here's the key; instruct the heads of all departments that each year for the next seven years their budget will be cut off 5% and that no reduction in services will be tolerated. Those leaders who are successful in cutting their budgets while continuing the current service levels will receive a bonus at the end of the seven years equal to one year's salary."

"And those who don't or say they can't?"

"If they can't do it we will find someone who can. Those not up to the task can seek employment elsewhere but there will be no golden parachutes."

"Wow. So you really think we can cut the entire Federal budget by 30% and not reduce services?"

"Private companies are asked to do it all the time. You'd be surprised with how creative and resourceful people can become when the options are reward on one hand and a pink slip on the other. But you know, the deeper problem lies in why voters choose their Congressmen and why Congress continues to spend. Benjamin Franklin and Alexis De Tocqueville both saw the possibility of this day coming, I can't remember right off hand which one said what but their two quotes go something like this:

"I believe this Republic shall stand until the politicians realize they can bribe the voters with their own money."

"And then from the other perspective:"

"This Republic shall be strong until the people realize they can vote themselves a raise."

"I submit to you that both these things have already happened. Politicians promise programs and spending that will benefit voters in each election and the promises continue to mount. Conversely, voters are too quick to elect politicians based upon what the candidate is promising. It's a never ending cycle. And that's how you end up twenty trillion dollars in debt. The Federal budget each year has a pie graph which shows where all the money is spent. Three programs, count them, three programs receive over 60% of the entire Federal budget." Gordon began naming the three programs on his fingers: "Medicare, Medicaid and Social Security." There was a pause.

"Well over half the budget goes to just three programs?"

"Yes. You could eliminate defense, education, NASA, the park system, the FDA, the IRS, the FBI, everything else and still not balance the budget."

"Wow."

Tim lost his smile and turned to the camera. "Back in a few." Russert turned back towards Gordon. "You are freaking kidding me!"

"Nope. It gets worse, as baby boomers get older and more retire, Medicare and Social Security will expand even more. It won't be long before those three programs eat up 70% of the entire Federal budget."

"Good god."

Tim sat in stunned silence as he considered the numbers. The red light returned. "Colonel, please share those numbers with our viewers." Gordon obliged. "So fight one big budget battle rather than hundreds of little ones?"

"Yes."

"But how do you get Congress to go along?"

"They must be incentivized as well. There should be a monetary reward at the end of the seven years."

"They should be rewarded for doing their job?"

"I didn't say they had to take it. Those who view it as repugnant can return it to the treasury to pay towards the debt. And let's consider for a moment what happens even in year one of 5% cuts. When Wall Street sees an actual reduction in spending and realizes Congress is serious about working towards a balanced budget I believe the stock market will take off like a rocket. Each year that the budget drops 5% stocks will get a boost which will cause everyone's 401-K to increase which would make voters very happy."

"Yes it would." Tim retrieved his smile. "Another topic; foreign trade."

"Match the tariffs, or lack thereof that other countries place on our products. A sort of do unto others as they do unto us philosophy."

"Now that was short and sweet. Immigration."

"Those who can contribute to our society, who have a marketable skill, and are free of communicable diseases, who have a full record of immunizations, who have never committed a felony should be allowed in our country. As long as you meet these criteria the path to citizenship should be quick and inexpensive. Now the numbers of annual recipients is up to negotiation based upon the needs of the workforce."

"What about our southern border?"

"It should be secured, but we need scores of low and median skilled workers who now cross our border illegally. We should place a series of migrant worker application centers along the border where applicants can receive a health screening, any needed immunizations, a skills assessment and the opportunity to be matched with an employer who needs their skill set. Workers would receive a yellow work card which could be renewed annually as long as they commit no felony and remain employed. They are not citizens and cannot vote, they can apply for citizenship though."

"Gun control."

"The right of the people to keep and bear arms, shall not be infringed."

"There goes that pesky constitution again."

Gordon laughed. "You can't selectively pick and choose only what you agree with. The whole document is law… With that said, I agree there is a problem in our country. I have no problem with a homeowner having a weapon… Or two, to defend his or her property or with hunters rights, but I do have a problem with those who would commit violent crime having the ability to kill tens or hundreds of people simply because they have the resources to pull it off. The genie is already out of the bottle. There are more guns in America then there are people and simply passing a law banning or limiting guns does nothing. Criminals don't obey the law. We don't have a gun problem as much as we have an ammunition problem. Give a bad guy a bunch of handguns, a thousand rounds of ammunition and you've got carnage. Give that dude the same handgun but only give him six bullets for personal protection and you have vastly reduced the outcome. If you want to make something illegal, make it illegal for each person to possess more than six rounds at a time.

"Just six?"

"Yep. You want six more? Bring your empty shell casings in and buy six more."

"What about the NRA?"

"The constitution protects your right to own weapons, it says nothing about ammunition."

"So Congress can simply restrict the amount of ammunition?"

"In my opinion, yes. We would need to seek international treaties banning the black market sale of ammunition, but that should be doable. And think about it, if you need to defend yourself, six shots for you, six shots for your wife, six shots for each of the kids should do it."

"Make it a whole family affair."

"So to speak."

"Global warming."

"Another hot topic for me. As an Eagle Scout and someone who loves nature, I've spent much of my life enjoying and cherishing our world. It is a gift and we must protect our planet as if our lives depended on it, because they obviously do. I do not question that the Earth has gone through numerous cycles of cooling and warming and I do not dispute that emissions and pollutants in general should be kept at the lowest levels possible. I mean, it's common sense; clean air is better than dirty air. Clean water is better than dirty water. A clean landscape is better than a dirty landscape. I am in complete agreement. Where I differ is in the assertion that America is the great offender in this equation, that we, as a country, are killing the earth and single-handedly causing global warming. In terms of carbon emissions the number one offender is China. They produce on average twice the carbon emissions that the United States does. In fact, China produces almost one third of the entire world's emissions. Now think about it, if your goal was to limit greenhouse gasses shouldn't you go to the by far greatest producer of these gasses? Yet I see no protests against China, just protests against America. In the last fifty years the U.S. has done the following, just to name a few: banned lead in our gasoline, banned lead in our paint, mandated catalytic converters in all gas-powered automobiles, mandated scrubbers in all coal-fired power plants, banned much open burning, greatly increased restrictions on all emissions, greatly increased miles-per-gallon standards, initiated country-wide recycling efforts, the list can go on and on. The point being, America has made great strides in reducing air, water and land pollutants and we continue to do more every day. I would suggest that those who want to prevent global warming may want to refocus their efforts to the world's number one polluter."

Tim reached out and Shook Gordon's hand. "Colonel, it has been both a pleasure and an honor."

"Thank you sir, I feel the same way."

Tim looked into the camera with a satisfied smile. "A civil and important conversation with one of our nation's true heroes... Colonel Gordon Alexander Hightower. I'm Tim Russert and this has been Meet the Press." The red light faded away and Tim leaned back into his chair. "Colonel, I can't tell you how much I enjoyed that. It was truth with no self-serving spin. A rarity I assure you.

"My pleasure, the Constitution speaks for itself."

A week after his appearance on "Meet the Press," Gordon pulled his car into his driveway and put the gear-shift into park. He turned off the ignition and made his way into his home. The phone was ringing so he put the bag of groceries onto the kitchen table and picked up the receiver. "Hello?"

"Colonel Hightower please."

"You got 'em."

"Colonel Hightower, my name is Woody Archer and I am the head of the Virginia state Republican Party, have you got a moment?"

"Sure, what's up?"

"Let me first say thank you for your service."

"You're very welcome."

"And let me also say that it is an honor to speak to a true American hero."

"Thank you, never really thought of myself as a hero, but thanks all the same."

"Colonel, I've been following your story over the past month and I loved your appearance on Meet the Press. The purpose of my call is to see if you would have a few moments that we could sit down and discuss an idea I have."

" Well, can you tell me what you have in mind?"

"Are you aware there is a movement to start a national right-in campaign to elect you for President?"

"You're kidding…"

"No sir, there are already 100,000 signatures and growing."

"Nobody's asked me."

"That's my fear, other people trying to generate this huge groundswell of support and then come to you with signatures in hand and try to… How shall I say it… Help you to negotiate the process. A sort of power behind the throne scenario."

"I see."

"Do you have some time this week we could sit down and talk?"

"Yeah, sure. Saturday for dinner?"

"How about Sunday?"

"Sure, that works. Time and place?"

"There's a pub down from the capitol on C street called Bull Feathers, ever heard of it?"

"Sure, ate there a couple years back."

"Awesome, how about 7:00 PM?"

"Sounds good."

"Thank you Colonel." Gordon hung up the receiver. It would be the most important phone call he would ever take.

Gordon walked into the venerable D.C. pub and looked around the dining room, Woody said he'd be wearing a navy blue blazer and from a corner table he saw a tall gentleman with salt and pepper hair stand and wave. The blue blazer worked well with the light yellow golf shirt. Gordon walked over and shook the lawyer's hand. "Colonel Hightower, it's a pleasure."

"Thanks, the pleasure's all mine."

The two men sat down, looked at the menu and made their selections when the waiter returned with their drinks. It was' Mason/Dixon' night and the two specials were a Boston clam chowder and a Charleston fried green tomato BLT with homemade pimento cheese. Woody went Northern and Gordon stayed in the South. After some small talk, Woody got to the reason for the meeting. "In your wildest dreams, do you think you're ready to run for president?"

"Absolutely not."

"Agreed. The jackals in this town would eat you for supper. People are excited to have someone they can believe in but Washington power is not given up easily. Candidates for president are bought and paid for in advance. It would not end well."

Gordon washed down his bite of sandwich. "I think we are in agreement that a draft Hightower movement is a no-go. So what's your idea?"

Woody put down his spoon and secretly wished he'd gotten the BLT. "President, Vice President, Governor, they are all out of the question. Senator… That's a reach too, but Congressman… Now that has a nice ring to it."

Gordon took a sip of ice-water with lemon and looked the Republican in the eye. "Really?"

"Yep… Seems we have a bit of serendipity right in your home district. Our current candidate failed to mention a little tax issue that's about to hit the press." Woody crumbled some more crackers into his soup. "People tend to not vote for tax cheats."

As was his custom, Gordon wore his full dress uniform. He stood in the wings just out of view of the 2000 people that had jammed into the ballroom of the local Hilton. Congressional acceptance speeches are typically made before a few hundred supporters… But not tonight. On this second Tuesday in November it was a standing room only occasion and was being covered by every national news service known to man. He checked his left breast pocket to make sure his backup copy of his speech was there… This teleprompter thing took a bit of getting used to. The event manager gently grasped his right arm. "Ten seconds Colonel."

"Thanks."

Woody raised a fist in the air in triumph, looked over at his new friend and shouted into the microphone… "Ladies and gentlemen, please welcome, Congressman Gordon Hightower!"

A huge cheer rose from the crowd as Gordon quickly walked to the lectern. The two men exchanged a generous handshake and Woody exited the stage. A chant of "Gordie! Gordie! Gordie!" started in the back and worked its way to the front. Gordon turned a bright shade of pink and beamed at the chant. He took a sip of water and held up his hand to quieten the crowd. He smiled a bit as he looked up at Peg and touched his heart. Colonel Gordon Alexander Hightower addressed his supporters and began to give the speech of his life.

"Considered by many to be just a plain ol' common man, Abraham Lincoln distinguished himself in a decade that was unparalleled in turmoil throughout all of American history. He was assigned the unenviable task of uniting two regions divided by belief systems which can only be described as being as different as night and day.

Throughout his over four years in this country's highest office, Mr. Lincoln showed, by example, that a politician's highest call is that of maintaining honesty, integrity and dignity when in service to the people. Abraham Lincoln, in many ways, WAS a simple, common man. He once said, 'God must love the common man, 'cause he made so many of 'em.' He believed that the common man was the thread, which held together this marvelous patchwork quilt we call America.

Mr. Lincoln received less than a year of formal education, yet he graduated Summa Cum Laude in the school of life. For it was in the hallowed halls of childhood that Lincoln learned the secrets to earning the respect of his peers; keep your word, promise only what you can deliver, finish what you start, and refuse to be bought.

He believed that a life devoid of honor was a life soon to find ruin. He felt that the common man had the RIGHT to place a higher calling upon his elected officials, and to expect them to carry out their duties in a selfless, honest and devoted manner.

Ladies and gentlemen, this is in essence why we are here today. Many of the men and women whom the people have chosen to serve us have fallen short of this higher calling. We find ourselves saddled with a federal government, which finds itself powerless to correct the problems, which face our great land.

As I look to our nation's capital, I find no Lincolns, no Jeffersons, no Washingtons, no Franklins. I find instead a never-ending parade of self-serving politicians who prefer to bankrupt the economy of this great land rather than make the difficult choices which they face daily. Choices, which would pale in significance when compared with the choices President Lincoln faced in 1861. Mr. Lincoln made these choices and preserved the Union. Today's bureaucrats side step the issues and often reward themselves with perks unavailable to the common man and sometimes exempt themselves from the very laws, which they force on you and I.

The noted European philosopher Alexis De Toqueville visited America in the 1800's and wrote upon his departure that: 'This American Republic will stand until the politicians realize that they can bribe the people with their own money.' Ladies and Gentlemen, I submit to you that that day has come. For when you ask people why they voted for a specific congressional candidate their answer will usually be topped by at least one government program which the Congressman helps them access. This, my friends, is evidence of how our federal government has fooled us into believing that without the help of Uncle Sam, our lives would never be as full. The very nation, which elected John Kennedy, NOW continually asks what their country can do for them. It is this nagging demon of governmental dependence, which we must forsake, the same way an alcoholic must forsake HIS demon known as alcohol.

I submit to you that there is a devious virus which has found its way into the halls of Congress, and most Congressmen have been susceptible to this highly contagious disease, a disease known as 'congressional coma', who's main symptom is paralysis of the conscience. Our task is to discover those Americans who have been inoculated with the vaccine called 'living in the real world'. For the only cure for congressional coma is a transfusion of new blood.

My friends, if you came here today because you love your country, then today is a milestone, for today we plant a seed. We plant a seed of patriotism in the hearts and minds of the people, which with nurturing will grow as mighty as a California Redwood.

Today we light a fire. An all-consuming flame, which burns white-hot with justice. A flame, which can only be doused by the murky water called complacency.

Today we start a great quest. A journey, which will make us soul mates with the likes of Jefferson, Washington and Franklin. For today we set a course towards revolution, a revolution to wrestle our government back from the hands of a few. A bloodless crusade, which will be won not by the musket, but by the ballot. Secured not by the cannon, but by the vote.

Today we raise the mantel of the people, which was passed down by the framers of this great land, which, to our shame, was laid aside somewhere in our forgotten past. This mantel, the right of the common man to self-determination, must be polished with hands filled with passion, virtue and patriotic zeal.

We stand in the shadow of a great bureaucratic wall. A wall so massive in proportions that it has far surpassed its intended purpose as a sea wall, meant to protect us in cases of emergency. Each new course of governmental brick threatens to rob our victory gardens of the sunlight that they need to survive. Federal lawmakers feel a sense of pride as they add new program and regulatory bricks to the wall, for each new brick represents a further enhancement of their power as Americans are drawn tighter into the spider's web called Big Government. This governmental wall has now become a spite fence that effectively separates the bureaucrat from the common man.

We are here to send a message to the Congressional and Executive branches of our government, a message from every Patriot from Kill Devil Hills to the island of Kauai. Listen up

Capital Hill, woe to you House of hypocrites, I've got a message from the common man; 'We're madder than hell and we ain't gonna' take it no more!'

We know that alone, the two-pound sledgehammers of our individual votes are no match for your great wall, but together, we've commandeered a bulldozer known to us all as, 'the American electorate'. And we are aiming that bulldozer headlong into your great spite fence and we will not stop until that edifice of your pride lies in a heap of glorious ruin. Then, we will reclaim those bricks that have merit and begin anew. All Americans are beckoned to this call. We need; carpenters, willing to hold the plumbline of truth. Masons, able to trowel out the political concrete of conviction. Accountants, able to balance the national ledger sheet and businessmen who KNOW the VALUE of a trillion dollars. For together, men and women of all trades and services will build a bulkhead which keeps at bay the sea of despair, yet lets in the light of capitalism to bathe us in its wealth.

It is to this call we assemble today, a people united in the single purpose of reclaiming our land. May God be with us and may we persevere till the end."